PRAYERS

of a Godly Woman

PRAYERS

of a *Godly* *Woman*

THIRD EDITION

Cover design & page layout by: Bart Dawson
Copy written and compiled by: Criswell Freeman

ISBN 1-58334-208-7

1 2 3 4 5 6 7 8 9 10 • 03 04 05 06 07 08 09 10

Printed in the United States of America

Contents

A Prayer for . . .

Introduction

Being a godly woman in today's world isn't easy. Never have expectations been higher, never have temptations been so plentiful, and never have demands been greater . . . and that's where God comes in. God stands ready, willing, and able to help us in every facet of our lives if we ask Him. But it is important to remember that the best way to ask God for His wisdom and His strength is to ask Him often.

Each day provides countless opportunities to praise God for His blessings. Yet sometimes, when the demands of life leave us exhausted or discouraged, we may fail to thank our Creator for His gifts. This book is intended to help.

You hold in your hands a text that contains 31 chapters, one for each day of the month. During the next 31 days, please try this experiment: read a chapter each day. If you're already committed to a daily worship time, this book will enrich that experience. If you are not, the simple act of giving God a few minutes each morning will change the direction and the quality of your life.

This collection of Bible verses, stories, quotations, and prayers is intended to remind you of the eternal promises that are found in God's Holy Word and of God's never-ending love for You. May these pages be a blessing to you, and may you, in turn, be a blessing to those whom God has seen fit to place along your path.

Day 1
A Prayer for . . .

God's Grace

For by grace you have been saved through faith,
and that not of yourselves; it is the gift of God,
not of works, lest anyone should boast.

Ephesians 2:8-9 NKJV

God's grace is not earned . . . thank goodness! To earn God's love and His gift of eternal life would be far beyond the abilities of even the most righteous woman. Thankfully, grace is not an earthly reward for righteous behavior; it is a blessed spiritual gift that can be accepted by believers who dedicate themselves to God through Christ. When we accept Christ into our hearts, we are saved by His grace.

The familiar words of Ephesians 2:8 make God's promise perfectly clear: It is by grace we have been saved, through faith. We are saved not because of our good deeds but because of our faith in Christ.

God's grace is the ultimate gift, and we owe to Him the ultimate in thanksgiving. Let us praise the Creator for His priceless gift, and let us share the Good News with all who cross our paths. We return our Father's love by accepting His grace and by sharing His message and His love. When we do, we are eternally blessed . . . and the Father smiles.

In your greatest weakness,
turn to your greatest strength, Jesus, and
hear Him say, "My grace is sufficient for you, for
My strength is made perfect in weakness"
(2 Corinthians 12:9 NKJV).

Lisa Whelchel

∞

So let us come boldly to the throne of
our gracious God. There we will receive
his mercy, and we will find grace
to help us when we need it.

Hebrews 4:16 NLT

∞

In the depths of our sin, Christ died for us.
He did not wait for persons to get as close
as possible through obedience to
the law and righteous living.

Beth Moore

∞

How beautiful it is to learn that grace isn't
fragile, and that in the family of God
we can fail and not be a failure.

Gloria Gaither

Lord, You have saved me by Your grace.
Keep me mindful that Your grace is a gift that
I can accept but cannot earn. I praise You
for that priceless gift, today and forever.
Let me share the Good News of Your grace with
my family, with my friends, and with a world
that desperately needs Your healing touch.
~ Amen ~

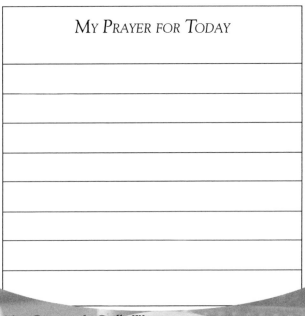

My Prayer for Today

Day 2
A Prayer for . . .

Make your ear attentive to wisdom,
incline your heart to understanding.

Proverbs 2:2 NASB

The ultimate source of wisdom is the Holy Word of God. If we call upon our Lord and seek to see the world through His eyes, He will give us guidance, wisdom, and perspective. When we make God's priorities our priorities, He will lead us according to His plan and according to His commandments. When we study God's Word, we are reminded that God's reality is the ultimate reality. But sometimes, when the demands of the day threaten to overwhelm us, we lose perspective, and we forfeit the blessings that God bestows upon those who accept His wisdom and His peace.

Do you seek to live according to God's plan? If so, you must study His Word. You must seek out worthy teachers and listen carefully to their advice. You must associate, day in and day out, with godly men and women. Then, as you accumulate wisdom, you must not keep it for yourself; you must, instead, share it with others.

But be forewarned: if you sincerely seek to share your hard-earned wisdom with the world, your actions must give credence to your words. The best way to share one's wisdom—perhaps the only way— is not by words but by example.

He who walks with the wise grows wise . . . .

Proverbs 13:20 NIV

∞

Knowledge can be found in
books or in school.
Wisdom, on the other hand,
starts with God . . . and ends there.

Marie T. Freeman

∞

This is my song through endless ages:
Jesus led me all the way.

Fanny Crosby

Lord, make me a woman of wisdom and
discernment. I seek wisdom, Lord, not as
the world gives but as You give. Lead me in
Your ways and teach me from Your Word
so that, in time, my wisdom might glorify
Your kingdom and Your Son.

~ Amen ~

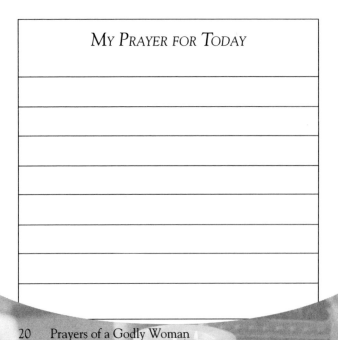

MY PRAYER FOR TODAY

Day 3

A Prayer for . . .

Stillness in the Presence of God

Be still, and know that I am God.

Psalm 46:10 KJV

We live in a noisy world, a world filled with distractions, frustrations, obligations, and complications. But we must not allow our clamorous world to separate us from God's peace. Instead, we must "be still" so that we might sense the presence of God.

If we are to maintain righteous minds and compassionate hearts, we must take time each day for prayer and for meditation. We must make ourselves still in the presence of our Creator. We must quiet our minds and our hearts so that we might sense God's love, God's will, and God's Son.

Has the busy pace of life robbed you of the peace that might otherwise be yours through Jesus Christ? If so, it's time to reorder your priorities. Nothing is more important than the time you spend with your Savior. So be still and claim the love and the peace that can be yours through Jesus Christ. It is yours for the asking. So ask. And then share.

Are you weak? Weary? Confused? Troubled?
Pressured? How is your relationship with God?
Is it held in its place of priority? I believe
the greater the pressure, the greater
your need for time alone with Him.

Kay Arthur

∞

Look around you and you'll be distressed;
look within yourself and you'll be depressed;
look at Jesus, and you'll be at rest!

Corrie ten Boom

∞

Be still before the LORD and
wait patiently for Him.

Psalm 37:7 NIV

∞

And he withdrew himself into the wilderness,
and prayed.

Luke 5:16 KJV

Dear Lord, let me be still before You;
let me feel Your presence; and let me sense
Your love. Amid the busyness of this day,
let me turn to You, Father, for comfort,
for assurance, and for peace.

~ Amen ~

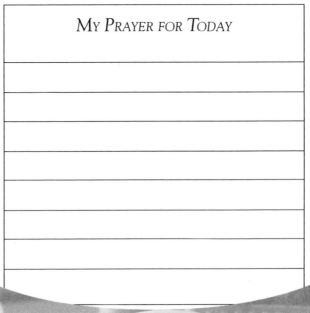

MY PRAYER FOR TODAY

Day 4
A Prayer for . . .

Spiritual Abundance

I am come that they might have life,
and that they might have it more abundantly.

John 10:10 KJV

The familiar words of John 10:10 should serve as a daily reminder: Christ came to this earth so that we might experience His abundance, His love, and His gift of eternal life. But Christ does not force Himself upon us; we must claim His gifts for ourselves.

Every woman knows that some days are so busy and so hurried that abundance seems a distant promise. It is not. Every day, we can claim the spiritual abundance that God promises for our lives . . . and we should.

Thomas Brooks spoke for believers of every generation when he observed, "Christ is the sun, and all the watches of our lives should be set by the dial of his motion." Christ, indeed, is the ultimate Savior of mankind and the personal Savior of those who believe in Him. As His servants, we should place Him at the very center of our lives. And, every day that God gives us breath, we should share Christ's love and His abundance with a world that needs both.

God is the giver, and we are the receivers.
And His richest gifts are bestowed not upon
those who do the greatest things, but upon
those who accept His abundance and His grace.

Hannah Whitall Smith

☙

If we were given all we wanted here, our hearts
would settle for this world rather than the next.

Elisabeth Elliot

☙

To those who use well what they are given,
even more will be given, and
they will have an abundance.

Matthew 25:29 NLT

☙

Ask and it will be given to you; seek and
you will find; knock and the door will be
opened to you. For everyone who asks receives;
he who seeks finds; and to him who knocks,
the door will be opened.

Matthew 7:7-8 NIV

Heavenly Father, thank You for
the abundant life that is mine through
Christ Jesus. Guide me according to Your will,
and help me to be a worthy servant in all that
I say and do. Give me courage, Lord, to claim
the spiritual abundance You have promised,
and when I do, let the glory be Yours.

~ Amen ~

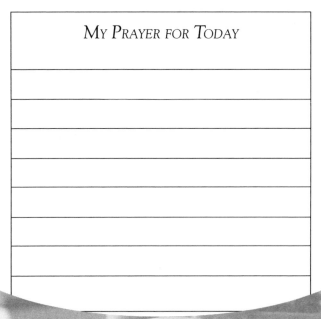

MY PRAYER FOR TODAY

Day 5

A Prayer for . . .

Patience

Rejoice in hope; be patient in affliction;
be persistent in prayer.

Romans 12:12 HCSB

Most of us are impatient for God to grant us the desires of our heart. Usually, we know *what* we want, and we know precisely *when* we want it: right now, if not sooner. But God may have other plans. And when God's plans differ from our own, we must trust in His infinite wisdom and in His infinite love.

As busy women living in a fast-paced world, many of us find that waiting quietly for God is difficult. Why? Because we are fallible human beings seeking to live according to our own timetables, not God's. In our better moments, we realize that patience is not only a virtue, but it is also a commandment from God.

God instructs us to be patient in all things. We must be patient with our families, our friends, and our associates. We must also be patient with our Creator as He unfolds His plan for our lives. And that's as it should be. After all, think how patient God has been with us.

The times we find ourselves having to wait
on others may be the perfect opportunities
to train ourselves to wait on the Lord.

Joni Eareckson Tada

∞

You're in a hurry. God is not. Trust God.

Marie T. Freeman

∞

Be completely humble and gentle; be patient,
bearing with one another in love.

Ephesians 4:2 NIV

∞

When I am dealing with an all-powerful,
all-knowing God, I, as a mere mortal, must offer
my petitions not only with persistence, but also
with patience. Someday I'll know why.

Ruth Bell Graham

Dear Lord, give me wisdom and patience.
When I am hurried, give me peace.
When I am frustrated, give me perspective.
When I am angry, keep me mindful of
Your presence. Today, let me be a patient
Christian, Lord, as I trust in You and
in Your master plan for my life.
~ Amen ~

MY PRAYER FOR TODAY

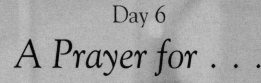

Day 6

A Prayer for . . .

A Cheerful Spirit

The cheerful heart has a continual feast.

Proverbs 15:15 NIV

Cheerfulness is a gift that we give to others *and* to ourselves. And, as believers who have been saved by a risen Christ, why shouldn't we be cheerful? The answer, of course, is that we have every reason to honor our Savior with joy in our hearts, smiles on our faces, and words of celebration on our lips.

Few things in life are more sad, or, for that matter, more absurd, than grumpy Christians. Christ promises us lives of abundance and joy *if* we accept His love and His grace. Yet sometimes, even the most righteous among us are beset by fits of ill temper and frustration. During these moments, we may not *feel* like turning our thoughts and prayers to Christ, but if we seek to gain perspective and peace, that's precisely what we must do.

Are you a cheerful Christian? You should be! And what is the best way to receive from Christ the joy that is rightfully *yours*? By giving Him what is rightfully *His*: your heart, your soul, and your life.

God knows everything. He can manage
everything, and He loves us.
Surely this is enough for a fullness of joy
that is beyond words.

Hannah Whitall Smith

∞

A cheerful heart is good medicine,
but a broken spirit saps a person's strength.

Proverbs 17:22 NLT

∞

Claim the joy that is yours. Pray. And know
that your joy is used by God to reach others.

Kay Arthur

∞

Jacob said, "For what a relief it is to see
your friendly smile. It is like seeing
the smile of God!"

Genesis 33:10 NLT

Dear Lord, Your Word reminds me that this is
the day that You have created; let me rejoice
in it. Today, let me choose an attitude of
cheerfulness and celebration. Let me be a joyful
Christian, Lord, quick to smile and slow to
anger. And, let me share Your goodness with
all whom I meet so that Your love might
shine in me and through me.

~ Amen ~

MY PRAYER FOR TODAY

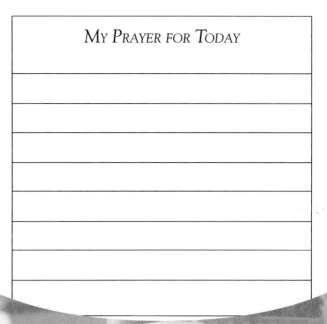

Day 7

A Prayer for . . .

This is the day which the LORD has made;
let us rejoice and be glad in it.

Psalm 118:24 NASB

This day is a gift from God. How will you use it? Will you celebrate God's gifts and obey His commandments? Will you share words of encouragement and hope with all who cross your path? Will you share the Good News of the risen Christ? Will you trust in the Father and praise His glorious handiwork? The answer to these questions will determine, to a surprising extent, the direction and the quality of your day.

The familiar words of Psalm 118:24 remind us of a profound yet simple truth: "This is the day which the LORD hath made; we will rejoice and be glad in it" (KJV). For Christian believers, every day begins and ends with God and His Son. Christ came to this earth to give us abundant life and eternal salvation. We give thanks to our Maker when we treasure each day and use it to the fullest.

Today, may we give thanks for this day and for the One who created it.

Today is mine. Tomorrow is none of
my business. If I peer anxiously into the fog
of the future, I will strain my spiritual eyes
so that I will not see clearly what
is required of me now.

Elisabeth Elliot

∞

Encourage one another daily,
as long as it is called Today . . . .

Hebrews 3:13 NIV

∞

Commitment to His lordship on Easter, at
revivals, or even every Sunday is not enough.
We must choose this day—and every day—
whom we will serve. This deliberate act of
the will is the inevitable choice between
habitual fellowship and habitual failure.

Beth Moore

∞

God gave you this glorious day.
Don't disappoint Him. Use it for His glory.

Marie T. Freeman

This is the day that You have given me, Lord.
Let me be thankful, and let me use it
according to Your plan. I praise You, Father,
for the gift of life and for the friends and family
members who make my life rich. Enable me to
live each moment to the fullest,
totally involved in Your will.
~ Amen ~

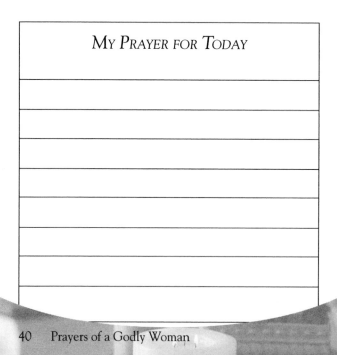

MY PRAYER FOR TODAY

My Hopes & Prayers for Next Week

My Hopes & Prayers for Next Week

Day 8

A Prayer for . . .

In thee, O LORD, do I put my trust.

Psalm 31:1 KJV

God has plans for each of us . . . important plans. To understand those plans, we must study God's Word and seek His will for our lives. When we do, He blesses us in ways that we, as mere mortals, could have scarcely imagined.

As believers, we know that we should trust God completely, but sometimes trusting Him is hard. When we reach the mountaintops of life, we find it easy to praise God and to give thanks. But, when we trudge through the dark valleys of bitterness and despair, trusting our Creator is more difficult. But trust Him we must.

Sometimes, God's plans may seem unmistakably clear to you. Other times, He may lead you through a deep valley before He directs you to the summit He has chosen. So be patient and keep seeking His will for your life. When you do, you'll be amazed at the marvelous things that an all-powerful, all-knowing God can do.

There is something incredibly comforting
about knowing that the Creator is
in control of your life.

Lisa Whelchel

∞

Anything is possible if a person believes.

Mark 9:23 NLT

∞

Is anything too hard for the LORD?

Genesis 18:14 KJV

∞

Just as our faith strengthens our prayer life,
so do our prayers deepen our faith.
Let us pray often, starting today,
for a deeper, more powerful faith.

Shirley Dobson

Dear Lord, I will earnestly seek Your will
for my life. You have a plan for me that I can
never fully understand. But You understand.
And I will trust You today, tomorrow,
and forever.

~ Amen ~

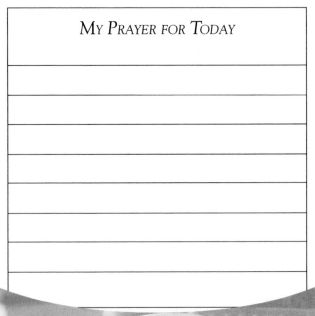

MY PRAYER FOR TODAY

Day 9
A Prayer for . . .

Renewal

Have you not known? Have you not heard?
The everlasting God, the LORD, the Creator
of the ends of the earth, neither faints nor is
weary. His understanding is unsearchable.
He gives power to the weak, and to those who
have no might He increases strength. Even
the youths shall faint and be weary, and
the young men shall utterly fall, but those who
wait on the LORD shall renew their strength;
they shall mount up with wings like eagles,
they shall run and not be weary,
they shall walk and not faint.

Isaiah 40:28–31 NKJV

God's Word is clear: When we genuinely lift our hearts and prayers to Him, He renews our strength. Are you almost too weary to lift your head? Then bow it. Offer your concerns and your fears to your Father in Heaven. He is always at your side, offering His love and His strength.

Are you troubled or anxious? Take your anxieties to God in prayer. Are you weak or worried? Delve deeply into God's Holy Word and sense His presence in the quiet moments of the early morning. Are you spiritually exhausted? Call upon fellow believers to support you, and call upon Christ to renew your spirit and your life. Your Savior will not let you down. To the contrary, He will lift you up *when* you ask Him to do so. So what, dear friend, are you waiting for?

He is the God of wholeness and restoration.
Stormie Omartian

∞

Jesus is calling the weary to rest,
Calling today, calling today,
Bring Him your burden and you shall be blest;
He will not turn you away.
Fanny Crosby

∞

Create in me a pure heart, O God, and renew
a steadfast spirit within me. Do not cast me
from your presence or take your Holy Spirit
from me. Restore to me the joy of your salvation
and grant me a willing spirit, to sustain me.
Psalm 51:10-12 NIV

Lord, I am an imperfect woman.
Because my faith is limited, I may become
overwhelmed by the demands of the day.
When I feel tired or discouraged, renew
my strength. When I am worried, let me turn
my thoughts and my prayers to You. Let me
trust Your promises, Dear Lord, and let me
accept Your unending love, now and forever.
~ Amen ~

MY PRAYER FOR TODAY

A Prayer for . . .

Contentment

I know what it is to be in need, and I know
what it is to have plenty. I have learned
the secret of being content in any and every
situation, whether well fed or hungry, whether
living in plenty or in want. I can do everything
through him who gives me strength.

Philippians 4:12-13 NIV

When we conduct ourselves in ways that are opposed to God's commandments, we rob ourselves of God's peace. When we fall prey to the temptations and distractions of our irreverent age, we rob ourselves of God's blessings. When we become preoccupied with material possessions or personal status, we forfeit the contentment that is rightfully ours in Christ.

Where can we find the kind of contentment that Paul describes in Philippians 4:12-13? Is it a result of wealth or power or fame? Hardly. Genuine contentment is a gift from God to those who follow His commandments and accept His Son. When Christ dwells at the center of our families and our lives, contentment will belong to us just as surely as we belong to Him.

Are you a contented Christian? If so, then you are well aware of the healing power of the risen Christ. But if your spirit is temporarily troubled, perhaps you need to focus less upon *your own* priorities and more upon *God's* priorities. When you do, you'll rediscover this life-changing truth: Genuine contentment begins with God . . . and ends there.

But godliness with contentment is great gain.
For we brought nothing into the world,
and we can take nothing out of it.
But if we have food and clothing,
we will be content with that.

1 Timothy 6:6-8 NIV

Those who are God's without reserve are,
in every sense, content.

Hannah Whitall Smith

Rejoicing is a matter of obedience to God—
an obedience that will start you on
the road to peace and contentment.

Kay Arthur

Keep your lives free from the love of money
and be content with what you have,
because God has said, "Never will I leave you;
never will I forsake you."

Hebrews 13:5 NIV

Dear Lord, You are my contentment
and my peace. I find protection when I seek
Your healing hand; I discover joy when
I welcome Your healing Spirit. Let me look to
You, Lord, for the peace and contentment
that You have offered me through
the gift of Your Son.

~ Amen ~

My Prayer for Today

Day 11

A Prayer for . . .

A Forgiving Heart

Do not judge, and you will not be judged.
Do not condemn, and you will not
be condemned. Forgive,
and you will be forgiven.

Luke 6:37 HCSB

Forgiveness is seldom easy, but it is always right. When we forgive those who have hurt us, we honor God by obeying His commandments. But when we harbor bitterness against others, we disobey God—with predictably unhappy results.

Are you easily frustrated by the inevitable shortcomings of others? Are you a prisoner of bitterness or regret? If so, perhaps you need a refresher course in the art of forgiveness.

If there exists even one person, alive or dead, whom you have not forgiven (and that includes yourself), follow God's commandment and His will for your life: forgive that person today. And remember that bitterness, anger, and regret *are not* part of God's plan for your life. Forgiveness is.

Forgiveness is the key that unlocks the door
of resentment and the handcuffs of hate.
It is a power that breaks the chains of bitterness
and the shackles of selfishness.

Corrie ten Boom

∞

Forgiveness is the precondition of love.

Catherine Marshall

∞

Be kind to one another, tender-hearted,
forgiving each other, just as God in Christ
also has forgiven you.

Ephesians 4:32 NASB

∞

You have heard that it was said,
"Love your neighbor and hate your enemy."
But I tell you: Love your enemies
and pray for those who persecute you.

Matthew 5:43-44 NIV

Lord, make me a woman who is slow to anger
and quick to forgive. When I am bitter,
You can change my unforgiving heart. And,
when I am angry, Your Word reminds me that
forgiveness is Your commandment. Let me be
Your obedient servant, Lord, and let me forgive
others just as You have forgiven me.

~ Amen ~

MY PRAYER FOR TODAY

Day 12

A Prayer for . . .

Friendships That Are Pleasing to God

Whoever walks with the wise will become wise;
whoever walks with fools will suffer harm.

Proverbs 13:20 NLT

Because we tend to become like our friends, we must choose our friends carefully. Because our friends influence us in ways that are both subtle and powerful, we must ensure that our friendships honor God. Because our friends have the power to lift us up or to bring us down, we must select friends who, by their words and their actions, encourage us to lead Christ-centered lives.

When we build lasting friendships that are pleasing to God, we are blessed. When we seek out encouraging friends and mentors, they lift us up. And, when we make ourselves a powerful source of encouragement to others, we do God's work here on earth.

Do you seek to be a godly Christian woman? If so, you should build friendships that honor your Creator. When you do, God will bless you *and* your friends, today and forever.

How good and pleasant it is when brothers
live together in unity!

Psalm 133:1 NIV

∞

Greater love has no one than this,
that he lay down his life for his friends.

John 15:13 NIV

∞

In friendship, God opens your eyes to
the glories of Himself.

Joni Eareckson Tada

∞

Beloved, if God so loved us,
we also ought to love one another.

1 John 4:11 NKJV

Lord, thank You for my friends.
Let me be a trustworthy friend to others,
and let my love for You be reflected
in my genuine love for them.
~ Amen ~

MY PRAYER FOR TODAY

Day 13

A Prayer for . . .

Obedience to God's Word

Therefore, get your minds ready for action,
being self-disciplined, and set your hope
completely on the grace to be brought to you
at the revelation of Jesus Christ. As obedient
children, do not be conformed to the desires
of your former ignorance but, as the One who
called you is holy, you also are to be
holy in all your conduct.

1 Peter 1:13-15 HCSB

Since God created Adam and Eve, we human beings have been rebelling against our Creator. Why? Because we are unwilling to trust God's Word, and we are unwilling to follow His commandments. God has given us a guidebook for righteous living called the Holy Bible. It contains thorough instructions that, if followed, lead to fulfillment, righteousness, and salvation. But, if we choose to ignore God's commandments, the results are as predictable as they are tragic.

Talking about God is easy; living by His commandments is considerably harder. But, unless we are willing to abide by God's laws, all of our righteous proclamations ring hollow.

How can we best proclaim our love for the Lord? By obeying Him. And, for further instructions, read the manual.

If you love Me, keep My commandments.

John 14:15 NKJV

∞

Our obedience does not make God any bigger
or better than He already is. Anything God
commands of us is so that our joy may be full—
the joy of seeing His glory revealed
to us and in us!

Beth Moore

∞

I seek you with all my heart . . . .

Psalm 119:10 NIV

∞

There is sharp necessity for giving Christ
absolute obedience. The devil bids for
our complete self-will. To whatever extent
we give this self-will the right to be master
over our lives, we are, to an extent,
giving Satan a toehold.

Catherine Marshall

Dear Lord, make me a woman who is obedient
to Your Word. Let me live according to
Your commandments. Direct my path far from
the temptations and distractions of this world.
And, let me discover Your will and follow it,
Lord, this day and always.

~ Amen ~

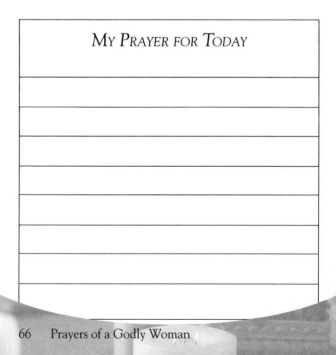

MY PRAYER FOR TODAY

Day 14

A Prayer for . . .

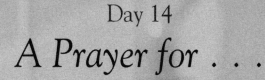

And now abide faith, hope, love, these three;
but the greatest of these is love.

1 Corinthians 13:13 NKJV

The familiar words of 1 Corinthians 13 remind us of the importance of love. Faith is important, of course. So too is hope. But love is more important still.

Christ showed His love for us on the cross, and, as Christians, we are called upon to return Christ's love by sharing it. We are commanded (not advised, not encouraged, but commanded!) to love one another just as Christ loved us (John 13:34). That's a tall order, but, as Christians, we are obligated to follow it.

Sometimes love is easy (puppies and sleeping children come to mind), and sometimes love is hard (fallible human beings come to mind). But God's Word is clear: We are to love all our neighbors not just the lovable ones. So today, take time to spread Christ's message by word and by example. And the greatest of these, of course, is example.

Love does no wrong to anyone,
so love satisfies all of God's requirements.

Romans 13:10 NLT

☾

It is when we come to the Lord in our
nothingness, our powerlessness, and our
helplessness that He then enables us to love
in a way which, without Him,
would be absolutely impossible.

Elisabeth Elliot

☾

Let love and faithfulness never leave you . . .
write them on the tablet of your heart.

Proverbs 3:3 NIV

☾

Love is the seed of all hope. It is the enticement
to trust, to risk, to try, and to go on.

Gloria Gaither

Dear God, let me share Your love with
the world. Make me a woman of compassion.
Help me to recognize the needs of others.
Let me forgive those who have hurt me,
just as You have forgiven me. And let the love
of Your Son shine in me and through me today,
tomorrow, and throughout all eternity.

~ Amen ~

MY PRAYER FOR TODAY

My Hopes & Prayers for Next Week

MY HOPES & PRAYERS FOR NEXT WEEK

Day 15

A Prayer for . . .

An Understanding Heart

But the wisdom that is from above is first pure,
then peaceable, gentle, willing to yield,
full of mercy and good fruits, without partiality
and without hypocrisy.

James 3:17 NKJV

W hat a blessing it is when our friends and loved ones genuinely seek to understand who we are and what we think. Just as we seek to be understood by others, so, too, should we seek to understand the hopes and dreams of our family members and friends.

We live in a busy world, a place where it is all too easy to overlook the needs of others, but God's Word instructs us to do otherwise. In the Gospel of Matthew, Jesus declares, "In everything, therefore, treat people the same way you want them to treat you, for this is the Law and the Prophets" (Matthew 7:12 NASB).

Today, as you consider all the things that Christ has done in your life, honor Him by being a little kinder than necessary. Honor Christ by slowing down long enough to notice the trials and tribulations of your neighbors. Honor Christ by giving the gift of understanding to friends and to family members alike. As a believer who has been eternally blessed by a loving Savior, you should do no less.

May the Lord cause you to increase
and abound in love for one another,
and for all people.

1 Thessalonians 3:12 NASB

∞

And be kind and compassionate to one another,
forgiving one another, just as God
also forgave you in Christ.

Ephesians 4:32 HCSB

∞

When we Christians are too busy to care
for each other, we're simply too busy
for our own good . . . and for God's.

Marie T. Freeman

Dear Lord, give me the patience
and the insight to understand my family
and my friends. Give me wisdom to speak
the right words to them, and give me
the courage to do the right things for them,
today and every day.

~ Amen ~

MY PRAYER FOR TODAY

Day 16

A Prayer for . . .

Family and Friends

And may the Lord cause you to increase
and overflow with love for one another
and for everyone, just as we also do for you.

1 Thessalonians 3:12 HCSB

A loving family is a treasure from God; so is a trustworthy friend. If you are a member of a close knit, supportive family, offer a word of thanks to your Creator. And if you have a close circle of trustworthy friends, consider yourself richly blessed.

Today, let us praise God for our family and for our friends. God has placed these people along our paths. Let us love them and care for them. And, let us give thanks to the Father for *all* the people who enrich our lives. These people are, in a very real sense, gifts from God; we should treat them as such.

You could have been born in another time and another place, but God determined to "people" your life with these particular friends.

Joni Eareckson Tada

∽

I thank my God every time I remember you.

Philippians 1:3 NIV

∽

A friend is always loyal, and a brother is born to help in time of need.

Proverbs 17:17 NLT

∽

Choose for yourselves this day whom you will serve . . . as for me and my household, we will serve the LORD.

Joshua 24:15 NIV

Dear Lord, I am part of Your family,
and I praise You for Your gifts and for Your love.
You have also blessed me with my earthly family
and friends, and I pray for them, that they
might be protected and blessed by You.
Let me show love and acceptance for others,
Lord, so that through me, they might come
to know You *and* to love You.
~ Amen ~

MY PRAYER FOR TODAY

A Prayer for . . .

The Power to Encourage Others

But encourage one another day after day,
as long as it is still called "Today," so that
none of you will be hardened by
the deceitfulness of sin.

Hebrews 3:13 NASB

Life is a team sport, and all of us need occasional pats on the back from our teammates. As Christians, we are called upon to spread the Good News of Christ, and we are also called to spread a message of encouragement and hope to the world.

In the Book of Ephesians, Paul writes, "Do not let any unwholesome talk come out of your mouths, but only what is helpful for building others up according to their needs, that it may benefit those who listen" (4:29 NIV). Paul reminds us that when we choose our words carefully, we can have a powerful impact on those around us.

Whether you realize it or not, many people with whom you come in contact every day are in desperate need of a smile or an encouraging word. The world can be a difficult place, and countless friends and family members may be troubled by the challenges of everyday life. Since we don't always know who needs our help, the best strategy is to encourage all the people who cross our paths. So today, be a world-class source of encouragement to everyone you meet. Never has the need been greater.

Let us consider how to stimulate one another
to love and good deeds.

Hebrews 10:24 NASB

∞

Encouragement starts at home,
but it should never end there.

Marie T. Freeman

∞

Kind words are like honey—
sweet to the soul and healthy for the body.

Proverbs 16:24 NLT

∞

Do not let any unwholesome talk come out
of your mouths, but only what is helpful for
building others up according to their needs,
that it may benefit those who listen.

Ephesians 4:29 NIV

Lord, because I am Your child, I am blessed.
You have loved me eternally, cared for me
faithfully, and saved me through the gift of
Your Son Jesus. Just as You have lifted me up,
Lord, let me also lift up others in a spirit of
encouragement and hope. And, if I can help
even a single person today, Dear Lord,
may the glory be Yours.

~ Amen ~

MY PRAYER FOR TODAY

Day 18

A Prayer for . . .

Assurance in Times of Change

Jesus Christ is the same
yesterday, today, and forever.
Hebrews 13:8 HCSB

Our world is in a state of constant change. God is not. At times, the world seems to be trembling beneath our feet. But we can be comforted in the knowledge that our Heavenly Father is the rock that cannot be shaken. His Word promises, "I am the LORD, I do not change" (Malachi 3:6 NKJV).

Every day that we live, we mortals encounter a multitude of changes—some good, some not so good. And on occasion, all of us must endure life-changing personal losses that leave us breathless. When we do, our loving Heavenly Father stands ready to protect us, to comfort us, to guide us, and, in time, to heal us.

Are you facing difficult circumstances or unwelcome changes? If so, please remember that God is far bigger than any problem you may face. So, instead of worrying about life's inevitable challenges, put your faith in the Father and His only begotten Son: "Jesus Christ is the same yesterday, today, and forever" (Hebrews 13:8 HCSB). And rest assured: It is precisely because your Savior *does not* change that you can face *your* challenges with courage for this day and hope for the future.

There is a time for everything,
and a season for every activity under heaven.

Ecclesiastes 3:1 NIV

∽

Often the trials we mourn are really gateways
into the good things we long for.

Hannah Whitall Smith

∽

Now glory be to God! By his mighty power
at work within us, he is able to accomplish
infinitely more than we would ever
dare to ask or hope.

Ephesians 3:20 NLT

∽

Measure the size of the obstacles
against the size of God.

Beth Moore

A PRAYER FOR TODAY

Dear Lord, our world changes,
but You are unchanging. When I face
challenges that leave me discouraged or fearful,
I will turn to You for strength and assurance.
Let my trust in You—like Your love for me—
be unchanging and everlasting.

~ Amen ~

MY PRAYER FOR TODAY

Day 19
A Prayer for . . .

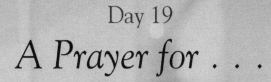

And there came a certain poor widow, and she threw in two mites, which make a farthing. And he called unto him his disciples, and saith unto them, Verily I say unto you, That this poor widow hath cast more in, than all they which have cast into the treasury . . . .

Mark 12:42-43 KJV

The thread of generosity is woven—completely and inextricably—into the very fabric of Christ's teachings. As He sent His disciples out to heal the sick and spread God's message of salvation, Jesus offered this guiding principle: "Freely you have received, freely give" (Matthew 10:8 NIV). The principle still applies. If we are to be disciples of Christ, we must give freely of our time, our possessions, and our love.

Lisa Whelchel spoke for Christian women everywhere when she observed, "The Lord has abundantly blessed me all of my life. I'm not trying to pay Him back for all of His wonderful gifts; I just realize that He gave them to me to give away." All of us have been blessed, and all of us are called to share those blessings without reservation.

Today, make this pledge and keep it: Be a cheerful, generous, courageous giver. The world needs your help, and you need the spiritual rewards that will be yours when you share your possessions, your talents, and your time.

The measure of a life, after all,
is not its duration but its donation.

Corrie ten Boom

∞

What is your focus today? Joy comes when it is
Jesus first, others second . . . then you.

Kay Arthur

∞

Freely you have received, freely give.

Matthew 10:8 NIV

∞

God loves a cheerful giver.

2 Corinthians 9:7 NIV

Dear Lord, Your Word tells me that it
is more blessed to give than to receive.
Make me a faithful steward of the gifts
You have given me, and let me share
those gifts generously with others,
today and every day that I live.

~ Amen ~

My Prayer for Today

Day 20

A Prayer for . . .

*Strength
and
Dignity*

Strength and dignity are her clothing,
and she smiles at the future. She opens
her mouth in wisdom, and the teaching of
kindness is on her tongue. She looks well
to the ways of her household,
and does not eat the bread of idleness.

Proverbs 31:25-27 NASB

God's Word reminds us again and again that our Creator expects us to lead disciplined lives. God doesn't reward laziness, misbehavior, or apathy. To the contrary, He expects believers to behave with dignity and discipline.

We live in a world in which leisure is glorified and indifference is often glamorized. But God has other plans. He did not create us for lives of mediocrity; He created us for far greater things.

Life's greatest rewards seldom fall into our laps; to the contrary, our greatest accomplishments usually require lots of work, which is perfectly fine with God. After all, He knows that we're up to the task, and He has big plans for us; may we, as disciplined believers, always be worthy of those plans.

The LORD is my strength and my song . . . .
Exodus 15:2 NIV

∞

God is our refuge and strength,
a very present help in trouble.
Psalm 46:1 NKJV

∞

Whatever your hand finds to do,
do it with all your might . . . .
Ecclesiastes 9:10 NIV

∞

And in truth, if we only knew it, our chief
fitness is our utter helplessness. His strength is
made perfect, not in our strength, but in our
weakness. Our strength is only a hindrance.
Hannah Whitall Smith

Dear Lord, let me turn to You for strength.
When I am weak, You lift me up.
When my spirit is crushed, You comfort me.
When I am victorious, Your Word reminds me
to be humble. Today and every day,
I will turn to You, Father, for strength, for hope,
for wisdom, and for salvation.

~ Amen ~

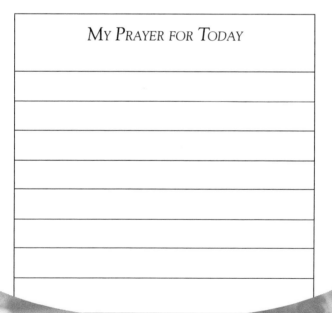

My Prayer for Today

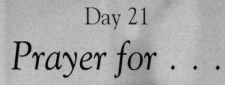

Day 21
Prayer for . . .

Wholeness

But Jesus turned him about, and when he saw
her, he said, Daughter, be of good comfort;
thy faith hath made thee whole. And the
woman was made whole from that hour.

Matthew 9:22 KJV

Until we have been touched by the Savior, we can never be completely whole. Until we have placed our hearts and our lives firmly in the hands of the living Christ, we are incomplete. Until we come to know Jesus, we long for a sense of peace that continues to elude us no matter how diligently we search.

Only God can make us truly whole. We can search far and wide for worldly substitutes, but when we seek peace apart from God, we will find neither peace nor God.

As believers, we are invited to accept the "peace that passes all understanding" (Philippians 4:7 NIV). That peace, of course, is God's peace. Let us accept His peace, and let us share it today, tomorrow, and every day that we live.

I am convinced our hearts are not healthy
until they have been satisfied by the only
completely healthy love that exists:
the love of God Himself.

Beth Moore

∽

And the peace of God, which surpasses every
thought, will guard your hearts and your minds
in Christ Jesus. Finally brothers, whatever is
true, whatever is honorable, whatever is just,
whatever is pure, whatever is lovely, whatever is
commendable—if there is any moral excellence
and if there is any praise—dwell
on these things.

Philippians 4:7-8 HCSB

∽

Those who love Your law have great peace,
and nothing causes them to stumble.

Psalm 119:165 NASB

∽

God is, must be, our answer to every question
and every cry of need.

Hannah Whitall Smith

Dear Lord, when I am broken, make me whole.
You sent Your perfect Son to save imperfect
people like me. I will welcome
the Prince of Peace into my heart
today, tomorrow, and forever.

~ Amen ~

My Prayer for Today

My Hopes & Prayers for Next Week

My Hopes & Prayers for Next Week

Day 22

A Prayer for . . .

Courage to Share the Good News

For I am not ashamed of this Good News
about Christ. It is the power of God at work,
saving everyone who believes.

Romans 1:16 NLT

In his second letter to Timothy, Paul shares a message to believers of every generation when he writes, "God has not given us a spirit of timidity" (1:7 NASB). Paul's meaning is crystal clear: When sharing our testimonies, we, as Christians, must be courageous, forthright, and unashamed.

We live in a world that desperately needs the healing message of Christ Jesus. Every believer, each in her own way, bears a personal responsibility for sharing that message.

If you are a believer in Christ, you know how He has touched your heart and changed your life. Now it is your turn to share the Good News with others. And remember: today is the perfect time to share your testimony because tomorrow may be too late.

What is courage? It is the ability to be
strong in trust, in conviction, in obedience.
To be courageous is to step out in faith—
to trust and obey, no matter what.

Kay Arthur

∞

Sing a new song to the LORD!
Let the whole earth sing to the LORD!
Sing to the LORD; bless his name. Each day
proclaim the good news that he saves.

Psalm 96:1-2 NLT

∞

Just pray for a tough hide and a tender heart.

Ruth Bell Graham

∞

Therefore, go and make disciples of all
the nations, baptizing them in the name of
the Father and the Son and the Holy Spirit.
Teach these new disciples to obey all
the commands I have given you.
And be sure of this: I am with you always,
even to the end of the age."

Matthew 28:19-20 NLT

Lord, You let me share the Good News of
Your Son. Jesus endured indignity, suffering,
and death so that I might live. Because He lives,
I, too, have Your promise of eternal life.
Let me share my faith with a world
that desperately needs Your healing hand
and the salvation of Your Son.

~ Amen ~

MY PRAYER FOR TODAY

Day 23

A Prayer for . . .

Trust in God's Promises

Let us hold on to the confession of
our hope without wavering,
for He who promised is faithful.

Hebrews 10:23 HCSB

What do you expect from the day ahead? Are you expecting God to do wonderful things, or are you living beneath a cloud of apprehension and doubt? The familiar words of Psalm 118:24 remind us of a profound yet simple truth: "This is the day which the LORD hath made; we will rejoice and be glad in it" (KJV).

For Christian believers, every day begins and ends with God's Son and God's promises. When we accept Christ into our hearts, God promises us the opportunity for earthly peace and spiritual abundance. But more importantly, God promises us the priceless gift of eternal life.

As we face the inevitable challenges of life here on earth, we must arm ourselves with the promises of God's Holy Word. When we do, we can expect the best, not only for the day ahead, but also for all eternity.

As for God, his way is perfect. All the LORD's
promises prove true. He is a shield for all
who look to him for protection.

Psalm 18:30 NLT

∞

We have ample evidence that the Lord
is able to guide. The promises cover every
imaginable situation. All we need to do
is to take the hand He stretches out.

Elisabeth Elliot

∞

Brother, is your faith looking upward today?
Trust in the promise of the Savior.
Sister, is the light shining bright on your way?
Trust in the promise of thy Lord.

Fanny Crosby

∞

When we are in a situation where Jesus
is all we have, we soon discover
He is all we really need.

Gigi Graham Tchividjian

Lord, Your Holy Word contains promises,
and I will trust them. I will use the Bible
as my guide, and I will trust You, Lord, to speak
to me through Your Holy Spirit and through
Your Holy Word, this day and forever.
~ Amen ~

My Prayer for Today

Day 24

A Prayer for . . .

Courage for
Difficult Days

Cast your burden upon the LORD
and He will sustain you: He will never allow
the righteous to be shaken.

Psalm 55:22 NASB

Women of every generation have experienced adversity, and this generation is no different. But, today's women face challenges that previous generations could have scarcely imagined. Thankfully, although the world continues to change, God's love remains constant. And, He remains ready to comfort us and strengthen us whenever we turn to Him.

Psalm 147 promises, "He heals the brokenhearted, and binds their wounds" (v. 3). When we are troubled, we must call upon God, and, in His own time and according to His own plan, He will heal us.

If you are like most women, it is simply a fact of life: from time to time, you worry. You worry about health, about finances, about safety, about relationships, about family, and about countless other challenges of life, some great and some small. Where is the best place to take your worries? Take them to God. Take your troubles to Him and your fears and your sorrows. Seek protection from the One who cannot be moved.

In all the old castles of England,
there was a place called the keep. It was always
the strongest and best protected place in the
castle, and in it were hidden all who were weak
and helpless and unable to defend themselves
in times of danger. Shall we be afraid to hide
ourselves in the keeping power of our Divine
Keeper, who neither slumbers nor sleeps, and
who has promised to preserve our going out and
our coming in, from this time forth
and even forever more?

Hannah Whitall Smith

∞

Be strong and courageous, and do the work.
Don't be afraid or discouraged by the size of
the task, for the LORD God, my God, is with
you. He will not fail you or forsake you.

1 Chronicles 28:20 NLT

∞

If a person fears God, he or she has no reason
to fear anything else. On the other hand,
if a person does not fear God,
then fear becomes a way of life.

Beth Moore

Lord, on difficult days, I will turn to You for
my strength. In times of sadness, I will put my
trust in You. In times of frustration, I will find
peace in You. And every day, whether I am
happy or sad, I will praise You for Your glorious
works and for the gift of Your Son.

~ Amen ~

MY PRAYER FOR TODAY

Day 25

A Prayer for . . .

Words That Are Pleasing to God

Let the words of my mouth, and the meditation of my heart, be acceptable in thy sight, O LORD, my strength and my redeemer.

Psalm 19:14 KJV

The words that we speak have the power to do great good or great harm. If we speak words of encouragement and hope, we can lift others up. And that's exactly what God commands us to do!

Sometimes, when we feel uplifted and secure, it is easy to speak kind words. Other times, when we are discouraged or tired, we can scarcely summon the energy to uplift ourselves, much less anyone else. God intends that we speak words of kindness, wisdom, and truth, no matter our circumstances, no matter our emotions. When we do, we share a priceless gift with the world, and we give glory to the One who gave His life for us. As believers, we must do no less.

Do not let any unwholesome talk come out
of your mouths, but only what is helpful for
building others up according to their needs,
that it may benefit those who listen.

Ephesians 4:29 NIV

∞

When you talk, choose the very same words
that you would use if Jesus were looking
over your shoulder. Because He is.

Marie T. Freeman

∞

If anyone considers himself religious and
yet does not keep a tight rein on his tongue,
he deceives himself and his religion
is worthless.

James 1:26 NIV

∞

Truthful lips endure forever,
but a lying tongue lasts only a moment.

Proverbs 12:19 NIV

Dear Lord, You have commanded me to choose
my words carefully so that I might be a source
of encouragement and hope to all whom I meet.
Keep me mindful, Lord, that I have influence
on many people. Let the words that
I speak today be worthy of the One
who has saved me forever.

~ Amen ~

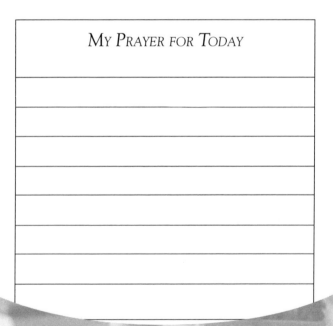

MY PRAYER FOR TODAY

Day 26
A Prayer for . . .

God's Peace

Peace I leave with you. My peace I give to you.
I do not give to you as the world gives.
Your heart must not be troubled or fearful.

John 14:27 HCSB

When we accept Jesus as our personal Savior, we are transformed by His grace. We are then free to accept the spiritual abundance and peace that can be ours through the power of the risen Christ.

The familiar and reassuring words of John 14:27 serve as a reminder that Jesus offers peace not as the world gives but as He alone gives.

As a gift to yourself, to your family, to your friends, and to the world, be still, trust God's Word, and claim the inner peace that is your spiritual birthright through Christ. It is a life-altering inner peace that is offered freely by your loving Savior. Accept it and share it today.

There may be no trumpet sound or loud
applause when we make a right decision,
just a calm sense of resolution and peace.

Gloria Gaither

∞

Come to me, all you who are weary
and burdened, and I will give you rest.
Take my yoke upon you and learn from me,
for I am gentle and humble in heart,
and you will find rest for your souls.
For my yoke is easy and my burden is light.

Matthew 11:28-30 NIV

∞

Thou wilt keep him in perfect peace,
whose mind is stayed on thee.

Isaiah 26:3 KJV

∞

To know God as He really is—in His essential
nature and character—is to arrive at a citadel of
peace that circumstances may storm,
but can never capture.

Catherine Marshall

Dear Lord, the peace that the world offers is
fleeting, but You offer a peace that is perfect
and eternal. Let me take my concerns and
burdens to You, Father, and let me feel
the spiritual abundance that You offer through
the person of Your Son, the Prince of Peace.

~ Amen ~

MY PRAYER FOR TODAY

Day 27

A Prayer for . . .

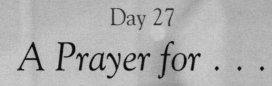

But grow in the grace and knowledge of our Lord
and Savior Jesus Christ. To Him be the glory,
both now and to the day of eternity.

2 Peter 3:18 NASB

The journey toward spiritual maturity lasts a lifetime. As Christians, we can and should continue to grow in the love and the knowledge of our Savior as long as we live. Norman Vincent Peale had the following advice for believers of all ages: "Ask the God who made you to keep remaking you." That advice, of course, is perfectly sound but often ignored.

When we cease to grow, either emotionally or spiritually, we do ourselves a profound disservice. But, if we study God's Word, if we obey His commandments, and if we live in the center of His will, we will not be "stagnant" believers; we will, instead, be growing Christians . . . and that's exactly what God wants for our lives.

I'm not what I want to be.
I'm not what I'm going to be.
But, thank God, I'm not what I was!

Gloria Gaither

∽

The disappointment has come not because God
desires to hurt you or make you miserable or
to demoralize you, or ruin your life, or keep you
from ever knowing happiness. He wants you to
be perfect and complete in every aspect, lacking
nothing. It's not the easy times that make you
more like Jesus but the hard times.

Kay Arthur

∽

It was he who gave some to be apostles, some to
be prophets, some to be evangelists, and some
to be pastors and teachers, to prepare God's
people for works of service, so that the body of
Christ may be built up until we all reach unity
in the faith and in the knowledge of the Son of
God and become mature, attaining to the whole
measure of the fullness of Christ.

Ephesians 4:11-13 NIV

Thank You, Lord, that I am not yet what
I am to become. The Holy Scripture tells me
that You are at work in my life, continuing
to help me grow and to mature in the faith.
Show me Your wisdom, Father, and let me live
according to Your Word and Your will.

~ Amen ~

MY PRAYER FOR TODAY

Day 28
A Prayer for . . .

A Thankful Heart

And let the peace of the Messiah,
to which you were also called in one body,
control your hearts. Be thankful.
Colossians 3:15 HCSB

Every good gift comes from God. As believers who have been saved by a risen Christ, we owe unending thanksgiving to our Heavenly Father. Yet sometimes, amid the crush of everyday living, we simply don't stop long enough to pause and thank our Creator for His countless blessings.

As believing Christians, we are blessed beyond measure. Thus, thanksgiving should become a habit, a regular part of our daily routines. God's gifts are too numerous to count, and we owe Him everything, including our eternal praise...starting now.

It is always possible to be thankful for what is given rather than to complain about what is not given. One or the other becomes a habit of life.

Elisabeth Elliot

∞

Enter his gates with thanksgiving,
go into his courts with praise.
Give thanks to him and bless his name.

Psalm 100:4 NLT

∞

I will thank you, LORD, with all my heart;
I will tell of all the marvelous things you have
done. I will be filled with joy because of you.
I will sing praises to your name, O Most High.

Psalm 9:1-2 NLT

∞

God is worthy of our praise and is pleased
when we come before Him with thanksgiving.

Shirley Dobson

Lord, let me be a thankful Christian.
Your blessings are priceless and eternal.
I praise You, Lord, for Your gifts and,
most of all, for Your Son. Your love
endures forever. I will offer You
my heartfelt thanksgiving this day
and throughout all eternity.
~ Amen ~

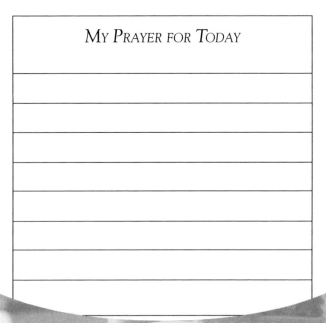

MY PRAYER FOR TODAY

MY HOPES & PRAYERS FOR NEXT WEEK

My Hopes & Prayers for Next Week

Day 29

A Prayer for . . .

Strength

I am able to do all things through Him
who strengthens me.

Philippians 4:13 HCSB

Have you "tapped in" to the power of God? Have you turned your life and your heart over to Him, or are you muddling along under your own power? The answer to this question will determine the quality of your life here on earth and the destiny of your life throughout all eternity.

The Bible tells us that we can do all things through the power of our risen Savior, Jesus Christ. But what does the Bible say about our powers outside the will of Christ? The Bible teaches us that "the wages of sin is death" (Romans 6:23). Thus our challenge is clear: we must place Christ where He belongs: at the very center of our lives. When we do so, we will surely discover that He offers us the strength to live victoriously in this world and eternally in the next.

My God is my rock, in whom I find protection.
He is my shield, the strength of my salvation,
and my stronghold, my high tower, my savior,
the one who saves me from violence.

2 Samuel 22:3 NLT

∽

We are never stronger than the moment
we admit we are weak.

Beth Moore

∽

The LORD is my rock, my fortress, and
my savior; my God is my rock, in whom I find
protection. He is my shield, the strength of
my salvation, and my stronghold.

Psalm 18:2 NLT

∽

Worry does not empty tomorrow of its sorrow;
it empties today of its strength.

Corrie ten Boom

A Prayer for Today

Lord, sometimes life is difficult. Sometimes,
I am worried, weary, or heartbroken. But, when
I lift my eyes to You, Father, You strengthen me.
When I am weak, You lift me up. Today,
I turn to You, Lord, for my strength,
for my hope, and my salvation.

~ Amen ~

My Prayer for Today

Day 30
A Prayer for . . .

Celebration

This is the day which the LORD has made;
let us rejoice and be glad in it.

Psalm 118:24 NASB

Life should never be taken for granted. Each day is a priceless gift from God and should be treated as such.

Hannah Whitall Smith observed, "How changed our lives would be if we could only fly through the days on wings of surrender and trust!" And Clement of Alexandria noted, "All our life is a celebration for us; we are convinced, in fact, that God is always everywhere. We sing while we work . . . we pray while we carry out all life's other occupations." These words remind us that this day is God's creation, a gift to be treasured and savored.

Today, let us celebrate life with smiles on our faces and kind words on our lips. After all, this is God's day, and He has given us clear instructions for its use. We are commanded to rejoice and be glad. So, with no further ado, let the celebration begin . . . .

Rejoice in the Lord always.
Again I will say, rejoice!
Philippians 4:4 NKJV

∞

Make a joyful noise unto the LORD,
all ye lands. Serve the LORD with gladness:
come before his presence with singing.
Psalm 100:1-2 KJV

∞

Praise Him! Praise Him!
Tell of His excellent greatness.
Praise Him! Praise Him!
Ever in joyful song!
Fanny Crosby

Lord God, You have given me so many reasons
to celebrate. The heavens proclaim Your
handiwork, and every star in the sky tells of
Your power. You sent Your Son to die for my
sins, and You gave me the gift of eternal life.
Let me be mindful of all my blessings,
and let me celebrate You and Your marvelous
creation. Today is Your gift to me, Lord.
Let me use it to Your glory.

~ Amen ~

MY PRAYER FOR TODAY

Day 31

A Prayer for . . .

Christ's Salvation

For God so loved the world that he gave his one
and only Son, that whoever believes in him
shall not perish but have eternal life.

John 3:16 NIV

Christ sacrificed His life on the cross so that we might have eternal life. This gift, freely given by God's only begotten Son, is the priceless possession of everyone who accepts Him as Lord and Savior. God is waiting patiently for each of us to accept the gift of eternal life. Let us claim Christ's gift today.

It is by God's grace that we have been saved, through faith. We are saved not because of our good deeds but because of our faith in Christ. May we, who have been given so much, praise our Savior for the gift of salvation, and may we share the joyous news of our Master's love and His grace.

The amazing thing about Jesus is that
He doesn't just patch up our lives,
He gives us a brand new sheet,
a clean slate to start over, all new.

Gloria Gaither

∽

It is by the name of Jesus Christ
of Nazareth . . . . Salvation is found in
no one else, for there is no other name
under heaven given to men
by which we must be saved.

Acts 4:10, 12 NIV

∽

I now know the power of the risen Lord!
He lives! The dawn of Easter has broken
in my own soul! My night is gone!

Mrs. Charles E. Cowman

∽

For by grace are ye saved through faith;
and that not of yourselves: it is the gift of God:
not of works, lest any man should boast.

Ephesians 2:8-9 KJV

Dear Lord, You have offered me the priceless
gift of eternal life through Your Son Jesus.
I accept Your gift, Lord, with thanksgiving
and praise. Today and every day, let me share
the Good News of my salvation with all those
who need Your healing touch.

~ Amen ~

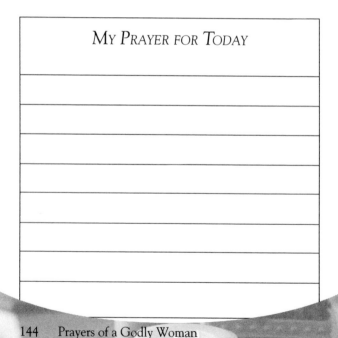

My Prayer for Today

MY HOPES & PRAYERS FOR NEXT MONTH

My Hopes & Prayers for Next Month

MY HOPES & PRAYERS FOR NEXT MONTH

My Hopes & Prayers for Next Month

_____

_____

_____

_____

_____

_____

_____

_____

_____

_____

_____

_____

_____

_____

_____

_____

_____

_____

_____

_____

Selected Scripture

Worry

Don't worry about anything; instead,
pray about everything. Tell God what you need,
and thank him for all he has done.
Philippians 4:6 NLT

⚭

Therefore do not worry about tomorrow,
for tomorrow will worry about itself.
Each day has enough trouble of its own.
Matthew 6:34 NIV

⚭

For this reason I say to you, do not be worried
about your life, as to what you will eat or
what you will drink; nor for your body, as to
what you will put on. Is not life more than food,
and the body more than clothing? Look at
the birds of the air, that they do not sow, nor
reap nor gather into barns, and yet
your heavenly Father feeds them.
Are you not worth much more than they?
Matthew 6:25-26 HCSB

Let not your heart be troubled;
you believe in God,
believe also in Me.

∞

John 14:1 NKJV

Anger

All bitterness, anger and wrath, insult and
slander must be removed from you, along with
all wickedness. And be kind and compassionate
to one another, forgiving one another,
just as God also forgave you in Christ.

Ephesians 4:31-32 HCSB

∽

A gentle answer turns away wrath,
but a harsh word stirs up anger.

Proverbs 15:1 NIV

∽

Stop your anger! Turn from your rage!
Do not envy others—it only leads to harm.

Psalm 37:8 NLT

∽

For he that will love life, and see good days,
let him refrain his tongue from evil,
and his lips that they speak no guile . . . .

1 Peter 3:10 KJV

Those who control their anger
have great understanding;
those with a hasty temper
will make mistakes.

∞

Proverbs 14:29 NLT

Love

Love is patient, love is kind and is not jealous;
love does not brag and is not arrogant,
does not act unbecomingly; it does not seek
its own, is not provoked, does not take into
account a wrong suffered, does not rejoice in
unrighteousness, but rejoices with the truth;
bears all things, believes all things,
hopes all things, endures all things.

1 Corinthians 13:4–7 NASB

∞

He who does not love does not know God,
for God is love.

1 John 4:8 NKJV

∞

And the most important piece of clothing you
must wear is love. Love is what binds us
all together in perfect harmony.

Colossians 3:14 NLT

∞

And now abide faith, hope, love, these three;
but the greatest of these is love.

1 Corinthians 13:13 NKJV

Love one another fervently
with a pure heart.

1 Peter 1:22 NKJV

Marriage

You wives must submit to your husbands,
as is fitting for those who belong to the Lord.
And you husbands must love your wives
and never treat them harshly.

Colossians 3:18-19 NLT

☙

Give honor to marriage, and remain faithful
to one another in marriage.

Hebrews 13:4 NLT

☙

Therefore shall a man leave his father
and his mother, and shall cleave unto his wife:
and they shall be one flesh.

Genesis 2:24 KJV

☙

Nevertheless, each individual among you
also is to love his own wife even as himself . . . .

Ephesians 5:33 NASB

Let love and faithfulness
never leave you . . .
write them on the tablet
of your heart.

∽

Proverbs 3:3 NIV

Hope

May the God of hope fill you with all joy and peace as you trust in him, so that you may overflow with hope by the power of the Holy Spirit.

Romans 15:13 NIV

∞

This hope we have as an anchor of the soul, a hope both sure and steadfast.

Hebrews 6:19 NASB

∞

I wait quietly before God, for my hope is in him.

Psalm 62:5 NLT

∞

Rejoice in hope; be patient in affliction; be persistent in prayer.

Romans 12:12 HCSB

But as for me,
I will always have hope;
I will praise you more and more.

∽

Psalm 71:14 *NIV*